I. INTRODUCTION

A. BACKGROUND

Historically, the Department of Defense (DOD) has taken one of two tracks when organizing to operate in a new warfare domain. The first track was taken in the domain of air. When looking at the formation of a force to fight in this domain, the Army created the Air Service in 1918, which became the Army Air Corps in 1926.[1] Following World War II, the National Security Act of 1947 not only restructured the foreign policy apparatus and military within the United States (U.S.) government but also created an independent Air Force.[2]

The second track was taken in the domain of space. With space operations beginning in the 1950s, and human travel to space in the 1960s, the foundation was laid for the establishment of space as the fourth warfare domain.[3] However, even after operating in this domain for nearly 60 years, a stand-alone "space force" still does not exist. The closest the DOD came was with the establishment of U.S. Space Command (USSPACECOM) in 1985 as a functional combatant command (COCOM).[4] USSPACECOM was responsible for coordinating the DOD use of space assets to provide missile warning, communications, navigation, weather, and imagery and signals intelligence until its disestablishment in 2002.[5] Following the deactivation of USSPACECOM, U.S. Strategic Command (USSTRATCOM) assumed the space mission within the DOD, with the Air Force as the Executive Agent for Space, under the Joint

---

[1] "History," accessed February 16, 2015, http://www.airforce.com/learn-about/history/part1/.

[2] *National Security Act of 1947*, Pub. L. No. 253 (1947).

[3] "Cyberwar: War in the Fifth Domain," July 1, 2010, http://www.economist.com/node/16478792.

[4] Connie Dillon, "Air Force Space Command's Roots Traced Back to the 1940s," *Air Force Space Command*, December 10, 2012, http://www.spacedaily.com/reports/Air_Force_Space_Commands_roots_traced_back_to_the_1940s_999.html.

[5] "United States Space Command," accessed January 30, 2015, http://www.globalsecurity.org/space/agency/usspacecom.htm.

Functional Component Command for Space (JFCC Space).[6] Each branch of the military is involved in space and conducts space operations, as well as coordinates operations via JFCC Space.[7]

In 2009, Secretary of Defense (SECDEF) Robert Gates ordered the creation of a subordinate unified command under USSTRATCOM that would focus on military cyberspace operations.[8] U.S. Cyber Command (USCYBERCOM) merged several components of the DOD's network security mechanism, and unified them at the command's Fort Meade headquarters. The memorandum further detailed that the commander of USCYBERCOM would also be the director of the National Security Agency (NSA).[9] While the command achieved full operational capability (FOC) in 2010, it will not be at full strength until 2016.[10] The responsibilities and mission of USCYBERCOM are discussed in Chapter IV.

In a recent U.S. Naval Institute *Proceedings Magazine* article, ADM James Stavridis, USN (Ret.), and David Weinstein, a former strategic planner at USCYBERCOM, argue for the creation of a stand-alone cyber force.[11] They claim that the military's tradition-oriented and inelastic nature make the military ill suited, as currently constructed, to command and control cyber forces. Everything from recruiting the wrong people to personnel grooming and fitness standards are held up as flawed to attract the kind of talent necessary to fight and win in cyberspace.[12] While debate

---

[6] William S. Moncrief, "Building a United States Space Force," *Army Space Journal*, Winter/Spring 2010, 37; "Joint Functional Component Command for Space (JFCC Space)," accessed January 30, 2015, http://www.stratcom.mil/factsheets/7/JFCC_Space/.

[7] "Joint Functional Component Command for Space," March 15, 2013, http://www.vandenberg.af.mil/ library/factsheets/factsheet.asp?id=12579.

[8] Robert M. Gates, *Establishment of a Subordinate Unified U.S. Cyber Command Under U.S. Strategic Command for Military Cyberspace Operations*, Secretary of Defense Memorandum (Washington, DC: Department of Defense, 2009).

[9] Ibid.

[10] "U.S. Cyber Command," accessed October 11, 2014, http://www.stratcom.mil/factsheets/2/Cyber_ Command/; "USCYBERCOMMAND Cyber Mission Force," 2013, http://www.safcioa6.af.mil/shared/ media/document/AFD-140512-039.pdf.

[11] James G. Stavridis and David Weinstein, "Time for a U.S. Cyber Force," *Proceedings Magazine*, accessed January 10, 2015, http://www.usni.org/magazines/proceedings/2014-01/time-us-cyber-force.

[12] Ibid.

regarding its effectiveness is premature, efforts to improve cyber operations capability are vital to ensuring the DOD is able to succeed in the execution of its cyber mission.

With the advent of the cyber domain as the fifth warfare domain, determining the proper command and control (C2) structure of DOD cyber efforts is crucial.[13] The idea to create a new military branch dedicated to cyber issues has gained traction, while USCYBERCOM has begun operations as a sub-unified command of USSTRATCOM focused on cyber issues.[14] Analyzing several structures for a cyber force, and the benefits and drawbacks of each, is critical to ensure it is properly organized in a coherent command structure.

B.   RESEARCH QUESTIONS

This thesis will answer the following questions.

- What are the benefits and drawbacks of various C2 structures in the cyber domain?

- What alternative C2 structures would be appropriate for the cyber force?

- What can be learned from past decisions to create a stand-alone force dedicated to a new warfare domain?

- What can be learned from past decisions to utilize a joint force approach dedicated to a new warfare domain?

C.   BENEFITS OF STUDY

Presenting cyber force command structure options will inform decision makers with respect to C2 of cyber forces. Relying on structures that fail to meet the needs of the U.S. military should not occur. By better understanding C2 options, policy-makers will be better able to determine the proper structure for cyber forces.

D.   SCOPE AND LIMITATIONS

This thesis examines three command structures and the benefits and drawbacks of each, as well as historical examples of command structures for new warfare domains. It

---

[13] "The Cyber Domain: Security and Operations," accessed February 16, 2015, http://www.defense.gov/home/features/2013/0713_cyberdomain/.

[14] Stavridis and Weinstein, "Time for a U.S. Cyber Force"; "U.S. Cyber Command."

will not cover desirable personnel traits or incentives and benefits for consideration in populating a cyber force. It will also not recommend any particular option. Instead, it will provide information that can serve as a basis for decisions regarding the proper structure of the cyber force.

E.   METHODOLOGY

The methodology used for this thesis consists of a literature review of relevant materials covering historical case studies, current C2 structures, and a proposed stand-alone organization with responsibility for DOD cyber forces. Analysis of this review focused on potential application to cyber C2 and how historical references could provide context to C2 of forces in the cyber domain.

F.   ORGANIZATION OF THESIS

Chapter II examines the historical case of the DOD determining the C2 model for air as a new warfare domain. It focuses on the evolution of air forces within the DOD from a branch of the Army to an independent Air Force. Chapter III deals with the DOD organization with respect to its space forces, and the DOD decision to forgo a separate space force. Chapter IV examines the historical application of experiences with the air and space domains, and how decisions regarding C2 of those domains could apply to future decisions regarding cyber C2. It also explores three command structures for cyber forces: the model in use with USCYBERCOM as a sub-unified command within USSTRATCOM, a modified joint structure with USCYBERCOM as a stand-alone functional COCOM, and finally, a notional stand-alone cyber force. Chapter V provides a summary of findings and suggestions for future work on the topic of C2 of cyber forces.

II.   AIR DOMAIN

This chapter examines decisions made by the United States when confronted with the need to operate in a newly accessible warfare domain. From the first flight of a heavier-than-air vehicle in 1903, the U.S. military was forced to adapt to operating in a new environment. Over a four-decade span, the United States evolved from an Army-centric air force to creating a flying branch, the U.S. Air Force (USAF), in 1947. The chapter will also look at why the USAF exists today, what roles it serves, and how the experience of creating the Air Force applies to the cyber domain.

A.   HISTORY

The idea of branches in the U.S. military comes from its foundations under the British as a colonial force, as well as each branches' focus on "a unique mission within the overall mission of U.S. security and peace."[15] Under the U.S. Constitution, Congress is charged, "To raise and support Armies…to provide and maintain a Navy."[16] To that end, President Washington appointed a Secretary of War and a Secretary of the Navy to oversee those departments as cabinet secretaries.[17] Based on the unique mission sets of each of the services, military branches exist to segregate the services into separate entities in order to focus their training and funding to carry out their missions in unique warfare domains. Thus, as militaries considered leveraging access to the air domain in the early 20th century, determining how to structure forces to fight in the air became important.

Aviation officially became a part of the U.S. military in 1909, with the Army receiving a purpose-built Wright aircraft, just six years after the first aircraft flight in

---

[15] Richard W. Stewart, ed., *American Military History Volume I: The United States Army and the forging of a Nation, 1775–1917* (Washington, DC: Center of Military History, 2005), 28; "U.S. Armed Forces Overview," accessed March 9, 2015, http://www.military.com/join-armed-forces/us-military-overview.html.

[16] U.S. Constitution, Article I, Section 8.

[17] William Gardner Bell, *Secretaries of War and Secretaries of the Army: Portraits and Biographical Sketches* (Washington, DC: Center of Military History, 2010), 2; "Secretaries of the Navy," accessed March 10, 2015, http://www.u-s-history.com/pages/h1225.html.

1903.[18] U.S. military aircraft began military service in the Army as part of the Army Air Service during World War I. Following the war, Air Service leaders, led by Brigadier General William Mitchell, began advocating for an independent air force.[19] They saw the Army's use of the Air Service as limiting the application of air power to a strictly ground combat support role.[20]

During World War I, the Air Service served primarily to provide reconnaissance, artillery surveillance, and limited ground combat support roles, and was limited to mainly daylight flight, due in great part to the relatively unsophisticated nature of its aircraft.[21] Airpower theories related to strategic bombing and innovative uses of the airplane to fight and win wars were superseded by the need to provide reconnaissance and air support to ground troops, as agreed to during a meeting between Army Chief of Staff General MacArthur and Chief of Naval Operations Admiral Pratt in January 1931.[22] The full application of capabilities, such as long-range bombing, air-to-air engagements, and troop transport provided by operating in the air took a backseat to the Army's desire to support ground troops.

Despite the successful creation of the British Royal Air Force (RAF) during World War I, "created for a single purpose—to defend the skies over Britain," the best U.S. air power advocates could achieve was to improve aviation's importance within the Army in the inter-war period, leading in 1926 to the creation of the Army Air Corps.[23] Several further reorganizations led to the creation of Army Air Forces (AAF) in June 1941, with responsibility "for operational training and development of air doctrine...in

---

[18] "U.S. Army Aviation Timeline," accessed January 5, 2015, http://www.army.mil/aviation/timeline/index.html.

[19] Herman S. Wolk, *Planning and Organizing the Postwar Air Force: 1943–1947* (Washington, DC: United States Air Force, Office of Air Force History, 1984), 11–12.

[20] Ibid., 6.

[21] Maurer Maurer, ed., *The U.S. Air Service in World War I* (Washington, DC: United States Air Force, Office of Air Force History, 1978), 38.

[22] Wolk, *Planning and Organizing the Postwar Air Force: 1943–1947*, 19.

[23] "Royal Air Force History: World War I," accessed March 12, 2015, http://www.raf.mod.uk/history/ww1.cfm; Wolk, *Planning and Organizing the Postwar Air Force: 1943–1947*, 6, 10.

addition supply the War Department with the 'basis for requirements of personnel, equipment, and stores to be furnished by arms and services to the Army Air Forces.'"[24]

While the experience of the British showed the value of having a separate service dedicated solely to the air domain, the lack of proximate war and relative American isolationism in the early 20th century were likely sufficient to prevent the creation of a U.S. air force. As World War I was mainly fought in close proximity to England, there was little threat of air operations against the United States. American isolationism would continue, even as World War II began, until 1941, when the United States was attacked by Japanese forces at Pearl Harbor. The combat experience of the AAF during World War II, technological improvements, such as long-range heavy bombers, long-range fighter escorts, high performance engines, and lightweight and strong metal construction, allowed the AAF to tackle new missions in an innovative manner.

During World War II, the military dedicated a great deal of manpower and effort to its postwar structure and force planning. Through World War II, both the Army (under the War Department) and the Navy were separate cabinet level departments. While a great deal of planning focused on creating a unified department to cover all defense-related activity, the elevation of air forces to a co-equal position with the Army and Navy was a point of focus for senior AAF leaders.[25]

Due to the close working relationship between Generals Eisenhower (Supreme Allied Commander, Europe during the war, then Army Chief of Staff after) and Spaatz (head of Strategic Air Forces in Europe during the war, then Commanding General of AAF and the first Chief of Staff of the Air Force after the war), General Eisenhower became a proponent of an independent Air Force.[26] General Eisenhower experienced first-hand the effects of massed air operations. The bombardment of German forces in order to prepare the beaches of Normandy for the D-Day Invasion, providing air cover

---

[24] United States Army, *Army Regulation 95-5, Army Air Forces* (Washington, DC: United States Army, 1941), para. 4(d) and 5(c), in Wolk, *Planning and Organizing the Postwar Air Force: 1943–1947*, 21–22.

[25] Herman S. Wolk, *Toward Independence: The Emergence of the U.S. Air Force 1945–1947*, Air Force History and Museums Program (Bolling AFB, DC: Air Force History Support Office, 1996), 10.

[26] Wolk, *Planning and Organizing the Postwar Air Force: 1943–1947*, 36.

for the invasion force, and the massive air drop of Army personnel in the enemy's rear area during the invasion all likely played a role in his support for an independent Air Force. As the Allied and Joint Commander for the invasion, he saw the success provided by using the U.S. military in a joint and mutually reinforcing fashion. Likely, as a result of his time in command, he became an advocate for a unified defense department, dedicated to defense of the United States, which became the DOD.

Unlike the leadership of the Army and AAF, the senior leadership of the Navy at the time was opposed to both a unified department, and an independent air branch. Their argument was that the Joint Chiefs of Staff (JCS) was sufficient to deconflict prioritization between the War and Navy Departments. Navy leaders feared "a distinct threat to the existence of the Fleet Air Arm and the Marine Corps."[27] While the senior leadership of the Army had come around to the idea of unification and an independent air branch, the Navy's resistance played a role in the delay of both unification and creation of the USAF.

The Navy's concern was not without cause, considering the experiences of the British Royal Navy when the RAF was created. At that time, Britain's Royal Navy lost its air element, which was merged with the RAF, creating a unified flying force under one branch of service. This was a decision the British would ultimately rescind in 1938, likely in response to the looming threat of war in Europe.[28] While U.S. Navy leadership focused on the Royal Navy's loss of its air arm after World War I, the British saw the error of taking fleet aviation away from their navy, a lesson the United States would likely have observed and learned from. U.S. Navy leadership fears regarding this point were probably unfounded in this respect.

U.S. Navy leadership was also of the opinion that unification would lead to one military officer being left to command the entirety of the military, which they saw as,

---

[27] Wolk, *Planning and Organizing the Postwar Air Force: 1943–1947*, 36.

[28] Ibid., 86; "Naval Aviation History and Fleet Air Arm Origins: History of Naval Aviation of the Royal Navy and the Commonwealth," accessed March 11, 2015, http://fleetairarmarchive.net/History/Index.htm.

"beyond the capacity of one man."[29] In light of the success of the JCS at coordinating the war effort, such a view was uninformed. No one person would be left to command all the U.S. military without assistance and guidance from senior leaders in the other branches.

As seen in the case of the Department of the Navy, having a Secretary of the Navy does require that individual to set aside the requirements and provisioning of the Marine Corps, which is also under the Secretary's purview. Whatever the disagreement, the Navy's resistance would be overcome by lessons learned from the military at war as to why air power deserved its own dedicated branch of service.

B.   WHY AN AIR FORCE?

The evolution of air operations from troop support mechanism to a dynamic force capable of a number of different combat missions made the decision to create a unique branch of service easier to accept among senior Army leaders. Leadership within the AAF that had long advocated for independence now had allies within Army leadership, and in President Truman.[30] Based on combat experience in World War I, and especially in World War II, senior military leaders saw the benefits of strategic bombing, fighter escorts, and a heavy lift capability to move large formations of troops over long distances in relatively short order. Pre-war notions of air power's relevance in combat were rendered obsolete by the experiences of the war.

While the Army successfully managed the AAF throughout the war, the growing relevance of the aforementioned broader missions required something more. As was the case after World War I, the Army likely would have cut research and development of aircraft in order to advance its ground forces. As can be seen in the technological advancement of aircraft and the growing uses for those aircraft, post-World War II, an air force unable to adapt and change would have put the United States at a great disadvantage with its chief post-war adversary, the Soviet Union. Having a separate air branch, able to test and develop new combat systems, would allow the United States to ensure its defense, while also improving the military's overall combat power.

---

[29] Wolk, *Planning and Organizing the Postwar Air Force: 1943–1947*, 87.

[30] Ibid., 98.

Additionally, the invention and use of nuclear weapons during World War II signaled a vast new mission for an air force.

1. The Nuclear Mission

The nuclear mission required massive bombers to haul weapons to targets across great distances, something the Navy would be unable to provide with its carrier aircraft being limited in size due to flight deck restrictions.[31] Furthermore, at the dawn of the nuclear age, the only delivery mechanism in existence for such weapons was the B-29 Superfortress, something over which the AAF had control.[32] Even after the advent of intercontinental ballistic missiles (ICBMs) and subsequent growth of the strategic nuclear forces in the 1950s, the Air Force maintained sole ownership of the U.S. military's nuclear mission.[33] The arrival of submarine launched ballistic missiles (SLBMs), and tactical nuclear weapons (i.e., those weapons with shorter delivery ranges or lower nuclear yield) in the 1960s did provide an opportunity for both the Navy and Army to take on nuclear roles, but the Air Force retained the majority of the strategic deterrence mission.

2. Airpower Strategy

The strategic nuclear mission, coupled with the strategic bombing campaign of German and Japanese cities during World War II, were the realization of Italian General Giulio Douhet's vision of air forces as a strategic tool capable of winning wars. Douhet, and those air power proponents citing his ideas, argued for air forces acting independently of ground and naval forces to bypass enemy forces, instead focusing attacks on the civilian population to decrease support for war, and thus achieve a strategic victory.[34] In the view of U.S. advocates of Douhet's vision for air power, an independent

---

[31] Herman S. Wolk, *The Struggle for Air Force Independence: 1943–1947*, Air Force History and Museums Program (Bolling AFB, DC: Air Force History Support Office, 1997), 244.

[32] Ibid., 133.

[33] "The First ICMBs," accessed March 11, 2015, http://www.britannica.com/EBchecked/topic/135 7360/rocket-and-missile-system/57336/The-first-ICBMs.

[34] Wolk, *Planning and Organizing the Postwar Air Force: 1943–1947*, iii, 10.

air force would be freed from the necessity to focus mainly on support to ground troops, and thus able to both develop aircraft and use them in pursuit of an airpower strategy.

Based on experiences in World War II, many in the United States, including senior AAF leaders, believed that large scale ground warfare "could now be relegated to the past."[35] In this respect, their view coincided with the views of Royal Air Force leadership at the time.[36] The shared combat experience and joint operations of the RAF and AAF during World War II showed the result of having an independent air force, able to plan and carry out strikes against the enemy's war support efforts at will. An air force tied solely to the needs of the Army would be restricted from operating in a manner of its choosing, able to pursue its own objectives and tasks in support of war efforts.

In this view, Douhet can be seen as somewhat akin to a Clausewitz, or a Mahan, in terms of his long-term influence on his particular warfare domain of interest. While not applicable only to ground warfare, Clausewitz concerned himself with the conduct of ground wars. That his theories on war apply to other domains show its relevance and importance. Similarly, Mahan serves as one of the early naval warfare theorists, one whose ideas continue to influence naval strategy, especially U.S. Navy strategy, to this day. It is in this tradition that Douhet continues to influence USAF leadership, who continue to stress the strategic nature of airpower, and argue that it is possible to win wars by aviation alone.[37]

Following President Truman's support, Congress finally began drafting the legislation that would ultimately become the National Security Act of 1947, creating the structure in place today. In addition to creating a unified DOD headed by a SECDEF, the Act also legally separated the Air Force from the Army, leading to the creation of a separate Department of the Air Force, and the USAF.[38] After nearly four decades and two world wars, the Air Force became a unique branch of service. In the case of the Air Force, it was the experience of air operations under the Army, and the limitations of that

---

[35] Wolk, *Planning and Organizing the Postwar Air Force: 1943–1947*, 40–41.

[36] Ibid., 41.

[37] "Our Mission," accessed March 11, 2015, http://www.airforce.com/learn-about/our-mission/.

[38] *National Security Act of 1947*, Pub. L. No. 253 (1947), Section 207, 9–10; Section 208, 10–11.

relationship mentioned previously, that ultimately won the argument in favor of the proponents of an independent air branch.

C.   RELATIONSHIP TO CYBER DOMAIN

As cyber warfare continues to evolve and grow in importance as a military mission, it is possible the mission could grow sufficiently to necessitate a dedicated force, as in the case of the Army-controlled air forces from 1909–1947. A cyber force with an expanded mission set, and the necessary tools to conduct independent operations in support of cyber objectives could support the argument to create a separate branch of service. Such a branch would be dedicated solely to the cyber domain, as occurred with the Air Force and its missions.

Although there are parallels between the strategic (i.e., nuclear) mission and the strategic nature of offensive cyber operations (OCO), clear definitions of the cyber mission is still at a very early stage. As seen with the Air Force's struggle for independence, creating a cyber force focused solely on the cyber domain will require sufficient justification as its mission evolves to necessitate taking the cyber mission from the individual services and beginning, and then growing, a dedicated force.

Creating a cyber force would not necessarily end the cyber missions of the services. Despite the fears of Navy leadership during the debate of forming the Air Force, the Navy did not lose its fleet air mission. In fact, each of the branches retains an aviation capability to support their unique missions. In the cyber domain, the services would still have responsibility for their own network defense and incident response. Some portion of their individual cyber operations would be turned over to an independent force, but this would likely not entirely end their missions in cyberspace.

What is more likely is an iterative approach to change, as seen with the gradual evolution from the Army Air Service serving in a supporting role, to a broader air mission requiring ever greater forces to succeed. In this approach, USCYBERCOM would gain more autonomy through structural changes, similar to how the Army Air Corps, and then the AAF were granted more independence to conduct operations, yet remained a part of the Army. The stand-alone force model mentioned above will be explored in greater detail in Chapter IV.

D.   SUMMARY

As examined in this chapter, the United State adjusted to operations in the air domain relatively slowly. While the U.S. military gained an aviation mission in 1909, it did not create a separate military branch dedicated to fighting in that domain until 1947, despite attempts to change the C2 structure. The Air Force remains an important part of the DOD today, and it is widely regarded as one of the best air forces in the world. That is a testament to its growth as a force, and the skill with which it executes its numerous missions. As the cyber domain matures, there could be some forcing event or decision to act that leads to the creation of a branch of service dedicated solely to the cyber domain, much as happened to the Air Force.

Chapter III serves as the counterpoint to the military's experience with the air domain. Although the DOD has operated in space for nearly 60 years, it remains a joint mission, executed by each branch of the military. The chapter examines how the U.S. military has chosen to operate in space, why the military chose its C2 construct, and will examine how the C2 structure of space forces relates to cyber forces.

THIS PAGE INTENTIONALLY LEFT BLANK

III. SPACE DOMAIN

This chapter examines decisions made by the United States when confronted with the need to operate in the space domain. The Soviet Union's launch of Sputnik in 1957 ushered in the space age, and was a forcing function that pushed the United States to accelerate its space program. Unlike of its response in the air domain, the United States has resisted creating a stand-alone space force in the 57 years of U.S. space operations; instead, the military considers space a joint domain.

A. HISTORY

The United States began operating in space with the launch of *Explorer 1* on January 31, 1958.[39] Manned U.S. space operations began May 5, 1961, with the successful launch and recovery of *Mercury-Redstone 3* and astronaut Alan B. Sheppard.[40] Prior to that point, U.S. space experiments focused on studying the layers of the atmosphere through a series of sounding rocket launches, beginning as early as 1945, in a joint project between the Jet Propulsion Laboratory and U.S. Army Ordnance.[41] These early suborbital experiments helped advance the U.S. space program, eventually leading to sustained U.S. space operations.

Even from these earliest tests, the U.S. military was heavily involved in the U.S. space program, as the military understood the advantages of operating in this new domain. The ability to overfly an enemy's territory, while not violating its sovereignty, was a great advancement in the ability to collect intelligence about enemy force disposition, location and type of bases, new weapons systems, and a host of other information. It also offered a new method for striking an adversary in war, as the invention of ICBMs allowed. These advancements also lowered the risk of losing aircraft

---

[39] "The First United States Satellite and Space Launch Vehicle," accessed January 6, 2015, http://history.nasa.gov/sputnik/expinfo.html.

[40] "Mercury: MR-3," accessed January 6, 2015, http://www-pao.ksc.nasa.gov/kscpao/history/mercury/mr-3/mr-3.htm.

[41] "Sounding Rockets," accessed March 10, 2015, http://history.nasa.gov/SP-4402/ch5.htm.

and pilots on reconnaissance missions, and allowed for peacetime surveillance of potential adversaries.

By the early 1950s, The Navy, Army, and Air Force all had individual space programs. The Air Force focused its early efforts (and cooperated heavily with the Central Intelligence Agency [CIA]) on reconnaissance programs to support the Air Force's Strategic Air Command (SAC) in its strategic nuclear mission against the Soviet Union by collecting photographic intelligence of SAC targets.[42] Concurrently, the Navy and Army joined efforts to research their own reconnaissance satellites. The Navy and Army roles were subsequently reduced by the establishment of the National Aeronautics and Space Administration (NASA) in July 1959, and by the Department of Defense Directive (DODD) 5160.32 of 1961, which, "made the Air Force responsible for the research, development, production, and deployment of space systems for all three services."[43]

As the Air Force refined its space mission, it added spaced-based infrared sensors to warn of Soviet ICBM launches in the late 1950s, and give advanced warning of a nuclear attack.[44] Following the shoot-down of Francis Gary Powers' U-2 over Soviet territory in 1960, the United States focused on using space as an intelligence collection medium via on-orbit satellites. This led to the creation of the National Reconnaissance Office (NRO) that same year.[45] With the creation of the NRO, the Air Force lost its position of authority with regard to reconnaissance satellites, as the NRO was tasked with developing satellites on behalf of the military and the intelligence community (IC).[46] The Air Force was charged to focus "on the launching and tracking of missiles, and the conduct of various military support missions including communications, missile early

---

[42] Joshua Boehm et al., "A History of United States National Security Space Management and Organization," Federation of American Scientists, accessed March 10, 2015, http://fas.org/spp/eprint/article03.html#22; "History," accessed March 12, 2015, http://www.stratcom.mil/history/.

[43] Ibid.; Morgan W. Sanborn, "National Military Space Doctrine," *Air University Review*, January–February 1977, http://www.airpower.maxwell.af.mil/airchronicles/aureview/1977/jan-feb/sanborn.html.

[44] Boehm et al., "A History of United States National Security Space Management and Organization."

[45] Ibid.

[46] Ibid.

warning, meteorology, navigation, and the detection of nuclear detonations on earth from space."[47]

This was the first indication of where C2 of space forces and assets was headed, with the Air Force as the DOD's Executive Agent for Space. It was reasonable to grant the Air Force the power to lead DOD space operations, given the number of missions it was already executing. As Executive Agent, the Air Force could oversee all DOD space procurement and operations. This increased efficiency, decreased redundant systems and missions, and allowed the Army and Navy to focus more on their missions in their traditional domains, while still allowing those services to procure space systems they required to execute their missions.

B.   WHY NOT A SPACE FORCE?

As the space mission grew, the Air Force continued to receive a greater portion of DOD funding for space programs, reaching as high as 90% of all DOD funding for space research by 1961.[48] DODD 5160.32 was updated in 1970 to allow for service-specific research, testing, and development with respect to space systems, with the Air Force in a supporting role as necessary.[49] But, as it has since the late 1950s, the DOD still considers the space domain a joint warfare domain. As Executive Agent for Space, the Air Force receives the bulk of space funding, and also requires a larger cadre of space operations personnel than the other services. Of the military's $6.2 billion space budget request for fiscal year 2015, the Air Force received $5.6 billion of the funding, and has over 40,000 personnel (active duty service members, civilians, and contractors) assigned to the Air Force Space Command (this includes 5,400 personnel assigned to 24th Air Force, the cyber force branch of the USAF), with approximately 34,600 dedicated to the space

---

[47] Curtis Peebles, *High Frontier: The United States Air Force and the Military Space Program*, Air Force History and Museums Program (Bolling AFB, DC: Air Force History Support Office, 1997), 15 in Boehm et al., "A History of United States National Security Space Management and Organization."

[48] Department of Defense Directive 5030.18, "DOD Support of National Aeronautics and Space Administrations," 99 in Boehm et al., "A History of United States National Security Space Management and Organization."

[49] Sanborn, "National Military Space Doctrine."

mission.[50] By way of comparison, the Army has 2,400 personnel (active duty personnel and civilians) assigned to space cadre billets, while the Navy has just 127 active duty personnel in space cadre billets, as well as 11 active duty astronauts.[51]

As in the arguments regarding a specialized force dedicated to combat in the air domain, a debate about the need to create a stand-alone space force within the DOD has been ongoing for at least two decades.[52] Numerous reports cite a variety of factors for the lack of long-term planning and strategy development with respect to the DOD space assets and strategy. Unlike in the case of the Air Force, no stand-alone space force acting to secure freedom of maneuver in space for U.S. use has been created to-date.[53] From its earliest operations in space, the U.S. military and the IC saw space as a medium for intelligence collection. As such, early space C2 organizations focused on launching and managing satellites to collect intelligence information.

The creation of USSPACECOM in 1985 sought to synchronize all U.S. space operations in a functional COCOM C2 construct, but the command was disestablished in 2002, its functions given over to USSTRATCOM.[54] This likely had to do with the fact that USSTRATCOM was already responsible for the strategic nuclear mission, so granting it authority over space assets, with the capability to warn of an impending nuclear attack, made sense, and USSPACECOM became JFCC-Space, a sub-unified command under USSTRATCOM.

---

[50] "United States Department of Defense Fiscal Year 2015 Budget Request Overview," accessed March 12, 2015, http://comptroller.defense.gov/Portals/45/Documents/defbudget/fy2015/fy2015_Budget_Request_Overview_Book.pdf, 6–1; "United States Air Force: Fiscal Year 2016 Budget Overview," accessed March 12, 2015, http://www.saffm.hq.af.mil/shared/media/document/AFD-150210-043.pdf, 18 (FY15 enacted); "Air Force Space Command Fact Sheet," accessed March 12, 2015, http://www.afspc.af.mil/library/factsheets/factsheet.asp?id=3649; "24th Air Force Fact Sheet," accessed October 17, 2014, http://newpreview.afnews.af.mil/24af/library/factsheets/factsheet.asp?id=15663.

[51] "Army Space Personnel Development Office Fact Sheet," accessed March 12, 2015, http://www.smdc.army.mil/FactSheets/ASPDO.pdf; "Navy Space Cadre," August 6, 2014, http://www.doncio.navy.mil/chips/ArticleDetails.aspx?ID=5356.

[52] Kurt S. Story, *A Separate Space Force: An Old Debate with Renewed Relevance* (Carlisle Barracks, PA: U.S. Army War College, 2002), 1; John D. Cinnamon, *U.S. Department of the Space Force: A Necessary Evolution* (Norfolk, VA: Joint Forces Staff College, 2012), 11; Leah Tanner, "A Cyber Force for U.S. Cyberspace Operations" (unpublished manuscript, September 17, 2014), 1–2.

[53] Mark E. Harter, "Ten Propositions Regarding Space Power: The Dawn of a Space Force," *Air & Space Power Journal*, Summer 2006, 76.

[54] USSTRATCOM, "History."

With space surveillance part of its purview, in 2005, USSTRATCOM stood up the Joint Functional Component Command for Intelligence, Surveillance, and Reconnaissance (JFCC ISR) in 2005, thus making it responsible to advocate for and apportion all aspects of intelligence, surveillance, and reconnaissance (ISR) to the geographic combatant commands (GCCs).[55] As can be seen, USSTRATCOM's role has grown, and it has taken on many different missions that provide strategic value to the U.S. military, including the two newest warfare domains, space and cyber. This was likely a result of improving DOD efficiency, as USSTRATCOM is a supporting commander to the other COCOMs. Rather than the other COCOMs having to reach out to several commands for assistance with operations and planning, the remaining COCOMs can work through a single functional COCOM. USSTRATCOM can act as a single point of contact for a host of mission-essential support functions, decreasing response time and helping COCOMs in need of support much more rapidly.

The disestablishment of USSPACECOM does not equate to decreased importance of space operations from a U.S. perspective. On the contrary, space is even more vital to U.S. interests than at any previous point in time, "The United States considers the sustainability, stability, and free access to, and use of, space vital to its national security interests."[56] Reliance on space for command and control purposes, communication, navigation, and many other factors has only increased.[57] As U.S. reliance on space has expanded, historical advantages have shrunk. Adversary nations increasingly are capable of impacting U.S. space operations. This provides U.S. adversaries with the potential to hinder terrestrial operations, a capability seen in the Chinese anti-satellite missile test of 2007, and foreseen in the 2012 *Joint Operational Access Concept*, "space and cyberspace

---

[55] "Joint Functional Component Command for Intelligence, Surveillance, and Reconnaissance (JFCC ISR)," accessed March 12, 2015, http://www.stratcom.mil/factsheets/6/JFCC_ISR/.

[56] Barack H. Obama, *National Space Policy of the United States of America* (Washington, DC: The White House, 2010), 3, http://www.whitehouse.gov/sites/default/files/national_space_policy_6-28-10.pdf.

[57] Department of Defense, *Joint Operational Access Concept (JOAC)* (Washington, DC: Department of Defense, 2012), 12, http://www.defense.gov/pubs/pdfs/JOAC_Jan%202012_Signed.pdf.

will be priority domains for many future adversaries, both state and non-state, because U.S. forces critically depend on them."[58]

More than ever, space assets are of critical importance to a broad spectrum of military operations, and USSTRATCOM fulfills its role as a supporting COCOM with a broad spectrum of capabilities, including space operations. Although C2 of space forces have changed constantly over nearly six decades, and regardless of any perceived advantages in creating a stand-alone space force, USSTRATCOM is more than capable of meeting challenges to U.S. space superiority, and ensuring continuity of U.S. space operations.

C. RELATIONSHIP TO CYBER DOMAIN

The arguments in favor of creating a space force parallel several of the arguments for a cyber force, and the relative advantage enjoyed by the United States in the cyber domain is similar to the early stages of space operations. The widely-cited lack of an overarching space strategy, lack of unified control over space forces, and difficulty countering adversary space activities are all similar to problems debated with respect to the cyber domain. Several proponents of a stand-alone cyber force allude to issues with C2 of cyber forces, lack of a cyber strategy, and adversary activity in cyberspace against the United States.[59]

While there are certainly issues with C2 of cyber forces, USCYBERCOM is in the process of filling out its various mission teams with trained personnel, and C2 of those forces will likely improve in the near-term. As for cyber strategy, just because it is

---

[58] Department of Defense, *Joint Operational Access Concept (JOAC)*, 12; Marc Kaufman and Dafna Linzer, "China Criticized for Anti-Satellite Missile Test," *Washington Post*, January 20, 2007, http://www.washingtonpost.com/wp-dyn/content/article/2007/01/18/AR2007011801029.html.

[59] David C. Hathaway, *Digital Kasserine Pass: The Battle Over Command and Control of DoD's Cyber Forces* (Washington, DC: Brookings Institute, 2011); Ben FitzGerald and Parker Wright, *Digital Theaters: Decentralizing Cyber Command and Control* (Washington, DC: Center for a New American Security, 2014), http://www.cnas.org/sites/default/files/publications-pdf/CNAS_DigitalTheaters_FitzGeraldWright.pdf; "U.S. Needs to Construct National Cyber Security Policy," February 15, 2015, http://www.businessinsurance.com/article/20150215/NEWS06/302159999/u-s-needs-to-construct-national-cyber-security-policy?tags=%7C302; Paul J. Pena, "Evolving Threats Demand an Evolving National Security Strategy," *Forbes*, February 19, 2015, http://www.forbes.com/sites/realspin/2015/02/19/evolving-threats-demand-an-evolving-national-security-strategy/.

not discussed openly does not prove nonexistence. There is likely a strategy, but due to the sensitive nature of the methods in use, it is likely classified, and thus not available to debate its merits or flaws. The same applies to adversary activity in cyberspace. As seen with the indictment of five Chinese citizens suspected of cyber espionage against the United States, and the publicity surrounding the alleged North Korean cyber attack against Sony, there is likely a very robust network of highly trained personnel countering U.S. adversaries in cyberspace. Again, just because it is not well known does not provide proof of one way or the other with respect to U.S. military cyber capabilities.

One key difference between the space and cyber domains is the 1967 Outer Space Treaty, which restricts all signatories from putting any nuclear weapons into orbit, basing them on any celestial body (e.g., the moon), or stationing weapons in space via any other means. Furthermore, the treaty prevents signatories from establishing any bases in outer space, testing weapons in space, or conducting military maneuvers on celestial bodies. Finally, the treaty does allow the use of military personnel to conduct scientific research for peaceful purposes, as well as the free exploration of space for the benefit of all mankind.[60]

There is no analogous treaty with respect to cyberspace, and the difference is critical. Offensive activity can originate in cyberspace, and the military is free, within policy and legal limits, to operate in the domain. Therefore, the restraints that apply to the space domain do not apply to the cyber domain, enabling U.S. military cyber operations. If the United States were to accede to a treaty limiting or preventing military use of cyberspace, the situation would potentially resemble the space domain.

The early phase of cyber operations (prior to the proclamation of a cyber domain by the DOD) seems to mirror that of space operations, in that different components of the cyber mission set belonged to a host of different organizations. In terms of space, missions fell to different commands. From a cyber perspective, organizations like the NSA, Joint Functional Component Command-Network Warfare (JFCC-NW, responsible

---

[60] U.S. Department of State, *Treaty on Principles Governing the Activities of States in the Exploration and Use of Outer Space, Including the Moon and Other Celestial Bodies* (Washington, DC: Department of State, 1967), http://www.state.gov/www/global/arms/treaties/space1.html.

for computer network attack [CNA]), and Joint Task Force-Global Network Operations (JTF-GNO, responsible for computer network defense [CND]) all had roles in cyberspace. Unlike space, the functions of the disparate organizations (other than the NSA) were brought together relatively quickly and tasked to USCYBERCOM, as opposed to nearly 30 years from the first U.S. space operations to the creation of USSPACECOM.

D.   SUMMARY

As seen in this chapter, C2 of space forces evolved over time. The one constant was the primacy of the Air Force with respect to space operations. While the Air Force has been the Executive Agent for Space for some time, C2 of space forces has remained a joint venture. In some respects, C2 in this domain mirrors that of the cyber domain. While USSPACECOM provided the space domain its own functional COCOM for a time, C2 in the space domain now falls to JFCC Space, which like USCYBERCOM, is a sub-unified command of USSTRATCOM.

Chapter IV examines how historical decisions regarding C2 of forces in new warfare domains applies to the cyber domain. It considers three separate C2 structures. The first is the current structure in operation today. The second is a functional COCOM, similar to USSOCOM, by removing USCYBERCOM from USSTRATCOM. The final structure is a stand-alone U.S. Cyber Force, as proposed by Stavridis and Weinstein, and mentioned earlier in this thesis.

IV.   COMPETING CYBER COMMAND STRUCTURES

This chapter examines historical applications of the air and space domains, and how those constructs would fit in a cyber C2 structure. It then considers three separate C2 structures for cyber missions, while highlighting some of the benefits and drawbacks to each. The three different C2 structures it examines are: 1) the existing structure, with USCYBERCOM as a sub-unified command under USSTRATCOM, and service cyber elements as the component commanders under USCYBERCOM, 2) a modified joint structure following the U.S. Special Operations Command (USSOCOM) model, with USCYBERCOM as a stand-alone functional COCOM and service elements providing cyber personnel to USCYBERCOM for tasking to support the GCCs, and 3) a stand-alone cyber force as a separate, co-equal branch of the military, responsible for all DOD cyber activities.

A.   HISTORICAL APPLICATION TO CYBER DOMAIN

With the declaration of cyberspace as an operational domain in 2011, cyber operations are at a relatively nascent stage when compared to the historical cases mentioned in this thesis.[61] The decision to spin-off the air domain from the Army into the Air Force took 38 years, while space operations continue as a joint function 57 years after U.S. space operations began. As these two domains have shown, time and planning are necessary to ensure successful C2 transitions. While the Air Force took nearly four decades to evolve from the Army Air Corps into the USAF, by proving the utility of full-spectrum air operations, independent air force advocates gained support for their vision. With regard to the space domain, numerous changes in C2 structure actually hampered effective C2 of space forces and assets. This resulted in more changes, before finally settling on the creation of JFCC Space, with the Air Force as the DOD's Executive Agent for space.

---

[61] David Alexander, "Pentagon to Treat Cyberspace as "Operational Domain,"" *Reuters*, July 14, 2011, http://www.reuters.com/article/2011/07/14/us-usa-defense-cybersecurity-idUSTRE76D5FA20 110714.

As it stands, USCYBERCOM is not fully manned at authorized levels and is completing force build out to reach its end-strength by 2016.[62] While a full examination of USCYBERCOM's effectiveness and ability to satisfy requirements cannot be complete until it is fully manned, there are different models to consider for cyber forces' C2 structure. In the historical cases mentioned in Chapters II and III, unique aspects of the air and space domains drove separate approaches that resulted in vastly different outcomes. When considering the cyber domain, it is instructive to look back and take stock of how the United States chose to organize its forces in the domains of air and space.

With respect to the cyber domain, the example of the space domain is more relevant today than that of the air domain. Not only is there no U.S. Cyber Force, both JFCC Space and USCYBERCOM are sub-unified commands under USSTRATCOM. Along with its other sub-unified commands, USSTRATCOM is well suited to fulfill its mission to, "Detect, deter, and prevent strategic attacks against the United States and our Allies," and is quite capable of doing so in the cyber domain.[63] While both space and cyber are warfare domains, the nature of operations in both domains is ill suited to an independent branch of the military. There is still the possibility that the evolution of the cyber mission could necessitate creation of a branch, but small changes to the C2 structure of cyber forces is more likely in the near term.

In terms of how the historical examples examined apply to the cyber domain, the case of the space domain mirrors that of the cyber domain, with the only distinction being the rapid evolution of C2 of cyber forces to match that of the space domain. With respect to C2 regarding the air domain, the outcome of modeling cyber C2 after that of the air would be a stand-alone branch of the military, focused solely on operations in the cyber domain. As in the case of the air domain, some cyber functions would remain with the services, and as each branch of service has an air arm, so too would each service have cyber operations specialists. If C2 of the cyber domain were to fall between the two

---

[62] "USCYBERCOMMAND Cyber Mission Force."

[63] "Mission," accessed March 12, 2015, http://www.stratcom.mil/mission/.

extremes, USCYBERCOM would become its own functional COCOM, similar to the space domain and USSPACECOM between 1985–2002.

What follows is an examination of each of the three C2 structures considered for purposes of this thesis. The current C2 structure of cyber forces is presented first.

B. CURRENT STRUCTURE

As currently constructed, USCYBERCOM is a sub-unified command that reports directly to the commander of USSTRATCOM, while each service has its own cyber element that falls both under the service and USCYBERCOM.[64] The mission statement for USCYBERCOM states that,

> USCYBERCOM plans, coordinates, integrates, synchronizes and conducts activities to: direct the operations and defense of specified Department of Defense information networks; and prepare to, and when directed, conduct full spectrum military cyberspace operations in order to enable actions in all domains, ensure U.S./Allied freedom of action in cyberspace and deny the same to our adversaries.[65]

In this role, USCYBERCOM is tasked with defending the Department of Defense Information Network (DODIN), providing support to the GCCs for mission execution, and improving the nation's ability to withstand and respond to cyber attacks. To execute these three focus areas, the command is standing up separate cyber mission teams dedicated to specific functions within the focus areas. The teams are, respectively, cyber protection forces (cyber protection teams—CPT), cyber combat mission forces (cyber mission teams—CMT), and cyber national mission forces (national mission teams—NMT).[66] To populate the teams, USCYBERCOM is determining the necessary team structure, training requirements, and necessary certification to allow for mission execution.[67] Figure 1 shows the current command structure. Personnel assigned to the service cyber ranks fall under the administrative authority of each of the services, while

---

[64] "U.S. Cyber Command."

[65] "USCYBERCOMMAND Cyber Mission Force."

[66] Ibid.

[67] "U.S. Cyber Command."

those assigned to USCYBERCOM fall under USCYBERCOM's authority. Combatant command and operational control over all cyber personnel resides with USCYBERCOM.[68]

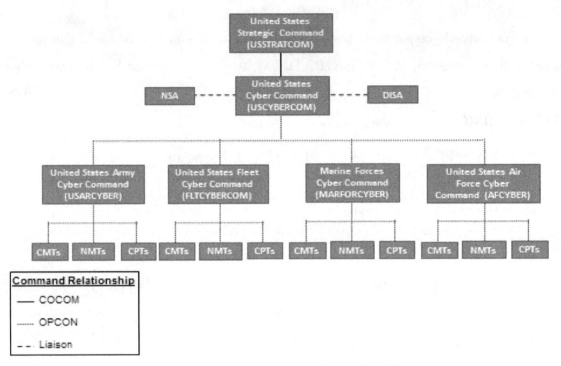

Figure 1.   Cyber Command Structure[69]

1.   Benefits of Current Structure

Since achieving FOC October 31, 2010, USCYBERCOM has been led by a four-star commander in a dual-hatted role with additional responsibilities as the Director of the National Security Agency/Central Security Service (NSA/CSS).[70] The decision to tie the commands together was based on the resident capability at the NSA's Fort Meade headquarters to conduct both computer network exploitation (CNE) and CNA (previously

---

[68] Duane Davis, "CY4400: Cyber Mission Planning" (lecture, Naval Postgraduate School, Monterey, CA: January 27, 2015).

[69] "U.S. Cyber Command."

[70] Gates, *Establishment of a Subordinate Unified U.S. Cyber Command Under U.S. Strategic Command for Military Cyberspace Operations.*

under the aegis of JFCC-NW). The relocation of JTF-GNO to Fort Meade in 2010 and subsequent disestablishment also brought the CND mission to USCYBERCOM.[71] In this dual-hatted setup, the USCYBERCOM and NSA head is responsible for both the DOD Title 10 authorities related to warfighting in cyberspace, and the IC Title 50 authorities related to signals intelligence (SIGINT) collection and exploitation.[72] Having the NSA and USCYBERCOM in the same location, with the same commander, provides the military with the unique capabilities of both commands, and improves both Title 10 and Title 50 support to the GCCs.

2. Drawbacks of Current Structure

One factor routinely cited by critics of the current command structure is the centrally controlled manner in which cyber forces and efforts are managed by USCYBERCOM. While the command is tasked with support for GCC missions worldwide, the distributed nature of the GCCs and the rigid control mechanisms in place are highlighted in several sources as a hindrance to the effective inclusion of cyber operations in GCC operational and planning efforts.[73] Various statements made in testimony before Congress by both former commander GEN Alexander, and current commander ADM Rogers, lead to confusion about how exactly the command intends to provide support to the GCCs. For example,

> DOD has at various points said that theater cyber will be 'under the command and control of whichever combatant command to which they are assigned', will be 'aligned under one of four Joint Force Headquarters-Cyber in direct support of geographic and functional combatant

---

[71] Gates, *Establishment of a Subordinate Unified U.S. Cyber Command Under U.S. Strategic Command for Military Cyberspace Operations*.

[72] James G. Stavridis and David Weinstein, "Divide and Conquer: Why Dual Authority at the NSA and Cyber Command Hurts U.S. Security," *Foreign Affairs*, October 23, 2013, http://www.foreignaffairs. com/articles/140206/james-g-stavridis-and-dave-weinstein/divide-and-conquer.

[73] Hathaway, *Digital Kasserine Pass: The Battle Over Command and Control of DoD's Cyber Forces*, iv; FitzGerald and Wright, *Digital Theaters: Decentralizing Cyber Command and Control*, 3.

commands', will 'work together with regional and functional commanders.'[74]

This very divide is the driving force behind many of the arguments (including that of ADM Stavridis and Mr. Weinstein) as to why the command structure of USCYBERCOM should change.[75]

Whether or not a decision is made to modify the C2 structure of cyber forces, based on the issues presented, it will be necessary to improve the coordination between assigned USCYBERCOM forces and the GCCs going forward if the command is to thrive as currently structured. As mentioned in this chapter, C2 of cyber forces currently most closely aligns with that found in the space domain. As C2 of space forces was improved to enhance space capabilities, the same is likely to occur with respect to C2 structures currently in place for cyber forces. As the military gains more experience in the cyber domain, it is likely to improve its efficiency and capabilities.

Next will be an examination of a modified joint structure, in the form of a USSOCOM C2 construct for cyber forces.

C.   MODIFIED JOINT STRUCTURE

The structure envisioned for a modified joint C2 model is heavily influenced by the work of Ben FitzGerald and Lt Col Parker Wright in *Digital Theaters: Decentralizing Cyber Command and Control* and Col David Hathaway in *The Digital Kasserine Pass: The Battle Over Command and Control of DOD's Cyber Forces*. FitzGerald and

---

[74] *Hearing on Strategic Command & Cyber Command Programs Before the Senate Committee on Armed Services*, 113th Congress (2014) (statement of General Keith B. Alexander, Commander, United States Cyber Command), http://www.armed-services.senate.gov/imo/media/doc/Alexander_02-27-14.pdf, 5; *Hearing on Strategic Command & Cyber Command Programs Before the Senate Committee on Armed Services*, 113th Congress (2013) (statement of General Keith B. Alexander, Commander, United States Cyber Command), http://www.armed-services.senate.gov/imo/media/doc/Alexander%2003-12-13.pdf, 6; *Advance Questions for Vice Admiral Michael S. Rogers, USN, Nominee for Commander, United States Cyber Command from the Senate Committee on Armed Services*, 113th Congress (2014), http://www. armed-services.senate.gov/imo/media/doc/Rogers_03-11-14.pdf, 14, in FitzGerald and Wright, *Digital Theaters: Decentralizing Cyber Command and Control*.
[75] Ibid.; Stavridis and Weinstein, "Divide and Conquer: Why Dual Authority at the NSA and Cyber Command Hurts U.S. Security."

Wright's operational control (OPCON) model envisions a structure similar to that of USSOCOM and its assignment of special operations forces (SOF) to the GCCs.[76]

Short of establishing a new military branch dedicated to the cyber realm, one possible alternative would be for the DOD to provide USCYBERCOM with more autonomy than it currently enjoys. When examining alternatives to the current command structure, one distinct possibility is the USSOCOM model.

USSOCOM's two-part mission is as follows, "Provide fully capable Special Operations Forces to defend the United States and its interests. Synchronize planning of global operations against terrorist networks." The command executes this mission across a broad scope of SOF core activities (direct action, special reconnaissance, security force assistance, etc.) and core operations (counterinsurgency, counterterrorism, support to major combat operations and campaigns, etc.).[77] A sampling of USSOCOM's Title 10 authorities and responsibilities include: develop special operations strategy, doctrine, and tactics; establish requirement priorities; ensure interoperability of equipment and forces; ensure SOF combat readiness; monitor SOF preparedness to carry out assigned missions; develop and acquire special operations-peculiar equipment, materiel, supplies, and services; and provide SOF to the GCCs.[78]

In contrast to the current C2 structure model, USCYBERCOM would be removed from its sub-unified position under USSTRATCOM and stand as its own functional COCOM. In this joint environment, each of the services would remain responsible for the man, train, and equip function of its cyber forces. Whether the dual-hatted nature of command of USCYBERCOM and the NSA continues in this construct would be an important decision point. At a minimum, USCYBERCOM would retain its Title 10 authorities and responsibilities for cyber missions, and would also be responsible to determine the requisite skills, training, and education necessary for its assigned joint service personnel.

---

[76] FitzGerald and Wright, *Digital Theaters: Decentralizing Cyber Command and Control*, 10.

[77] U.S. Special Operations Command, *USSOCOM Fact Book 2014* (MacDill AFB, FL: U.S. Special Operations Command, 2014), http://www.socom.mil/News/Documents/USSOCOM_Fact_Book_2014.pdf.

[78] Ibid.

1. Benefits of a Modified Joint Structure

By looking at the previously mentioned purpose, and the command structure of USSOCOM, it is easy to see a parallel to the cyber realm and imagine the command with a similar purpose tailored to the cyber mission set. Based on the specialized nature of personnel and training with respect to the cyber domain, a similarly scoped functional COCOM dedicated to cyber operations could mimic USSOCOM with success. Some of the functions brought about by following the USSOCOM model could include: improved streamlining of cyber response capabilities, improved cyberspace freedom of maneuver, rapid and covert employment of cyber support to GCC contingency plans, and dedicated mechanisms to fund cyber force initiatives. Figure 2 envisions a cyber C2 structure that follows the USSOCOM model.

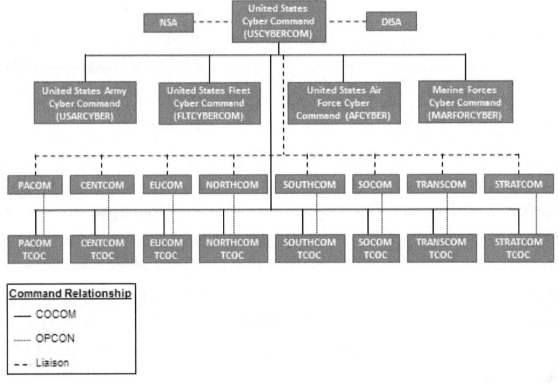

Figure 2.   Cyber Command Structure Using USSOCOM Model[79]

[79] U.S. Special Operations Command, *USSOCOM Fact Book 2012* (MacDill AFB, FL: U.S. Special Operations Command, 2012), http://www.socom.mil/News/Documents/USSOCOM_Fact_Book_2012.pdf.

Based on this structure, USCYBERCOM would provide its CMT personnel to each of the GCCs through a system similar to that of the SOF Theater Special Operations Commands (TSOCs). Each GCC has an assigned TSOC headed by a flag officer special operator who acts as the SOF component commander for the GCC. The TSOCs are a sub-unified command of USSOCOM, but OPCON of assigned forces is granted to the GCC by the SECDEF.[80]

A Theater Cyber Operations Command (TCOC), modeled after the TSOC construct, would allow the delegation of OPCON of assigned cyber forces to the GCC, which would potentially improve the support provided to the GCCs. Additionally, by co-locating the teams with their respective GCC, integration of cyber effects would likely improve, as the GCC would have daily interaction with its cyber element. With the regionally focused CMTs under operational control of the assigned GCC, the remaining CPTs and NMTs would remain co-located with USCYBERCOM and execute their particular missions from their assigned location.

2. Drawbacks of a Modified Joint Structure

While transitioning to this type of C2 structure would likely improve regional support to the GCCs, there are a series of drawbacks to shifting to such a model. The largest issue is the interconnected nature of cyberspace, and the fact that a regional focus to cyber operations would be counterintuitive. For example, while U.S. Central Command (USCENTCOM) may plan for a cyber operation in its region, the effects could impact other GCCs. This would require a number of personnel at each GCC to deconflict efforts among the GCCs, and with USCYBERCOM.[81]

The issue of collateral damage when conducting cyber operations also means authority to conduct operations would likely remain outside the control of the GCC, thus undermining the ability of the TCOC to support the GCC in a timely fashion.[82] The

---

[80] Chairman of the Joint Chiefs of Staff, *Joint Publication 3-05, Special Operations* (Washington, DC: Joint Chiefs of Staff, 2014), ix.

[81] Hathaway, *Digital Kasserine Pass: The Battle Over Command and Control of DoD's Cyber Forces*, 13.

[82] Ibid., 13–14.

TCOC would rely on USCYBERCOM for authority to conduct missions, "due to the potential for global collateral damage and the sensitivity of some cyber techniques, the execution authorities for many cyber operations will likely reside at USCYBERCOM at a minimum."[83] This scenario negates the benefit to the GCC of having OPCON over its assigned cyber forces. While partially solving the issues related to GCC support, this modified structure would present several new and challenging obstacles, as highlighted here.

3.   Application to the Cyber Domain

A change in policy, granting greater operational autonomy to USCYBERCOM would solve many of the issues expressed in this section. Due to political sensitivity regarding the use of offensive cyber measures, such autonomy is unlikely. Tight control over OCOs is likely to continue for the foreseeable future. While unlikely in the short term, such a change in policy would allow USCYBERCOM, either as currently structured, or as a functional COCOM, more freedom to operate. For all the faults expressed with a dedicated functional COCOM, shifting to a C2 structure based on a functional COCOM with responsibility for the cyber domain serves as a potential solution to many of the issues plaguing cyber support to the GCCs.

The final C2 structure to be examined in this chapter is the creation of a separate branch of the military, dedicated to the cyber domain.

D.   STAND-ALONE FORCE

Since his retirement, ADM James Stavridis has emerged as perhaps the strongest proponent of a force dedicated solely to the cyber domain. His growing interest in the cyber domain can be seen prior to his retirement when he argues that, "We need to understand this new cyber dimension of warfare and how to contend with it...military involvement is but a small piece of the puzzle...Thus, we need to continue to try to

---

[83] Robert E. Schmidle (Deputy Commander, USCYBERCOM, Fort Meade, MD), in Hathaway, *Digital Kasserine Pass: The Battle Over Command and Control of DoD's Cyber Forces*, 13.

understand cyber security in the larger interagency context."[84] Since retiring, he has released three separate articles advocating for improved military cyber awareness, including arguing for the creation of a stand-alone cyber force.[85] His main argument in favor of creating a dedicated cyber branch is to achieve more effective C2 of cyber forces. While improving C2 structures is important, creating such a force in itself would not solve challenges regarding support for the GCCs mentioned previously, nor would it solve all C2 issues. A stand-alone cyber force would require greater autonomy with respect to its operations that would be granted by a change in policy, just as in the cases of the current and modified joint structures mentioned previously.

A U.S. Cyber Force would require a command hierarchy similar to the other branches of the military, although almost certainly in more modest numbers than any single branch.[86] An analysis of mission and personnel requirements would be necessary to determine the proper number of cyber force personnel. As an historical comparison, the Air Force had just over 300,000 service members in 1947 at its founding, and over 309,000 today.[87] The authorized end strength as currently directed for USCYBERCOM is just over 6,000 billets (drawn from the services), while the services will by 2016 have nearly 43,000 total personnel (active duty service members, civilians, and contractors: Army: 21,000, Air Force: 5,400, Navy: 15,300, Marines: 1,000) dedicated to cyber missions, such as DODIN operations and offensive and defensive cyber operations

---

[84] James G. Stavridis, "Sailing the Cyber Seas," *Joint Forces Quarterly*, no. 65 (2nd Quarter 2012): 66, http://www.csl.army.mil/SLET/mccd/CyberSpacePubs/Sailing%20the%20Cyber%20Sea.pdf.

[85] Ibid., Stavridis and Weinstein, "Divide and Conquer: Why Dual Authority at the NSA and Cyber Command Hurts U.S. Security"; Stavridis and Weinstein, "Time for a U.S. Cyber Force."

[86] Tanner, "A Cyber Force for U.S. Cyberspace Operations," 6.

[87] Herman S. Wolk, *Reflections on Air Force Independence*, Air Force History and Museums Program (Bolling AFB, DC: Air Force History Support Office, 2007), 77; "Snapshot of the Air Force," accessed February 5, 2015, http://www.afpc.af.mil/library/airforcepersonneldemographics.asp.

(DCO).[88] While unlikely to be as large as the Air Force at its founding, a cyber force would likely be larger than the roughly 43,000 personnel envisioned by 2016.

1. Benefits of a Stand-Alone Force

By having a dedicated force focused solely on the cyber domain, such a service would be better able to build corporate knowledge than the constant two- to three-year rotation of new military personnel with little to no cyber experience currently allows, as highlighted in the Stavridis and Weinstein article,

> Perhaps surprisingly, the vast majority of CYBERCOM's military personnel are experiencing cyberspace for the first time in their careers. Helicopter pilots, chemical officers, B-2 navigators, tank drivers, infantry soldiers, and acquisition specialists occupy CYBERCOM's ranks. These personnel enter the cyber trenches at all levels of leadership with little to no related experience, so the command invests heavily in expensive training regimens to mitigate gaping proficiency holes. The long-term return on investment is strikingly minimal, however, as most personnel rotate out after three years to an entirely different discipline.[89]

What would such a force look like?

Establishing a cyber force as a separate service branch would require a service secretary to advise the President on military cyber operations, and a senior uniformed leader with membership on the JCS. Similar to the other military services, separate chains of command for administrative and operational purposes is necessary. A decision to maintain a singular chain of command would require changes in U.S. law, as the uniformed service leaders of the JCS are statutorily removed from the operational chain of command, serving in a strictly advisory role to the President and SECDEF.[90]

---

[88] "USCYBERCOMMAND Cyber Mission Force"; "24th Air Force Fact Sheet"; Cheryl Pellerin, "Marines Focused at Tactical Edge of Cyber, Commander Says," U.S. Department of Defense, June 10, 2013, http://www.defense.gov/news/newsarticle.aspx?id=120246; U.S. Fleet Cyber Command/U.S. Tenth Fleet, *U.S. Fleet Cyber Command/U.S. 10th Fleet 2014 Fact Sheet* (Ft. Meade, MD: U.S. Fleet Cyber Command/U.S. Tenth Fleet, 2014), http://www.public.navy.mil/fcc-c10f/Fact%20Sheets/FCC-C10F%20 Fact%20Sheet%202014.pdf; "Establishment of U.S. Army Cyber Command," accessed October 17, 2014, http://www.arcyber.army.mil/history_arcyber.html.

[89] Stavridis and Weinstein, "Time for a U.S. Cyber Force."

[90] Tanner, "A Cyber Force for U.S. Cyberspace Operations," 6.

34

Figure 3 is an attempt to depict what such a force could look like. It delineates the administrative and operational sides of the force, and is loosely based on the U.S. Navy's hierarchical model. The administrative and operational heads are responsible to the service chief and secretary for their particular functions. Commander, U.S. Cyber Forces would require liaison authority to interact with counterparts at the Department of Homeland Security (DHS) and the NSA.[91] This relatively familiar construct is similar to that of the existing branches of service, and would be familiar from a DOD perspective, potentially making such a drastic transition smoother than expected.

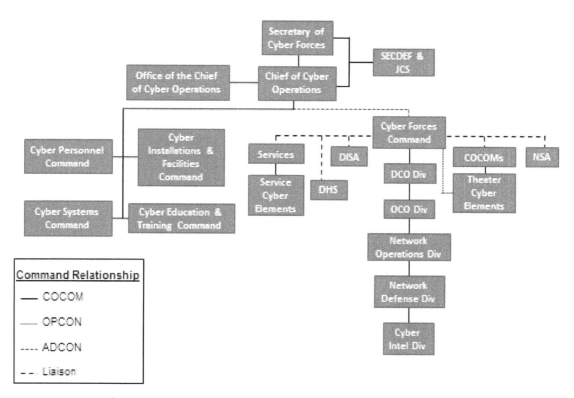

Figure 3.   Notional Cyber Force Command Structure[92]

2.   Drawbacks of a Stand-Alone Force

There are issues with the creation of a dedicated cyber force. One requirement to creating a stand-alone cyber force is building the necessary command structures and

---

[91] Tanner, "A Cyber Force for U.S. Cyberspace Operations," 6.

[92] "Navy Organization," accessed October 16, 2014, http://www.navy.mil/navydata/organization/org-top.asp.

bureaucracy to allow the force to function seamlessly with the four existing military branches. An entirely new hierarchy would need to be created, from the commander to the lowest-ranking cyber operator.[93] As in the example of the AAF splitting into an independent Air Force, personnel assigned to cyber billets would likely have a choice to join the cyber force at the time such a force is built,

> As to USAF personnel and functions, formerly under the Department of the Army or 'as are deemed by the Secretary of Defense to be necessary or desirable for the operations of the Department of the Air Force or the United States Air Force and the Department of the Air Force.'[94] For two years the Secretary of Defense should direct the movement of personnel, property, and installations from the Army to the Air Force.[95]

The issue of where to attract the necessary personnel from, and how best to manage them, is a complicating factor when discussing the creation of a stand-alone cyber force. While taking cyber personnel from the services and placing them in the cyber force would solve the immediate personnel needs, a dedicated training pipeline of some sort would be required to replenish, and potentially, grow the force. Additionally, the training mechanism would need to exist prior to any decision to shift personnel with cyber operations experience from the existing branches.

As enlistment contracts run out, or people choose to leave the service, the lack of ready replacements could leave significant weaknesses in military cyber operations. Depending on the personnel structure chosen, a system akin to the traditional services with numerous commissioning sources, including a dedicated Cyber Forces Service Academy, and an enlisted training program, might be necessary. The Army's recent decision to establish a cyber career field is an interesting example, and may prove an excellent template for cyber career management within the DOD.[96]

---

93 Tanner, "A Cyber Force for U.S. Cyberspace Operations," 1–2.

94 Hap Arnold, "Memo for Chief of Staff of the Army, December 4, 1945," in Wolk, *Planning and Organizing the Postwar Air Force: 1943–1947*, 174.

95 Wolk, *Planning and Organizing the Postwar Air Force: 1943–1947*, 173–174.

96 Fort Gordon Public Affairs Office, "Army Cyber Branch Offers Soldiers New Challenges, Opportunities," November 24, 2014, http://www.army.mil/article/138883/Army_Cyber_branch_offers_ Soldiers_new_challenges__opportunities/.

Finally, duplication of personnel and effort could be an issue. For context, the creation of the Air Force did not lead to an elimination of duplicative resources. Within the Department of the Navy, separate air branches still exist for both the Navy and Marine Corps. In fairness, the different air arms of each service have vastly distinct mission sets, requiring different functional platforms.

For example, the Marine Corps' air assets are employed for close air support and tactical transport of personnel and materiel. The Air Force's mission focuses on air and space superiority, global attack, rapid global mobility, precision engagement, information superiority, and agile combat support.[97] The number of aircraft in the four services highlights the problem of duplication, as the creation of a cyber force would likely require each service to retain residual cyber capabilities to operate and defend service-specific networks.[98]

E.   COMPARISON OF ALTERNATIVES

The distinct elements of each C2 model examined highlight the inherent benefits and drawbacks. Maintaining the current structure allows for continuity of policy and methods with minimal disruption to operations; however, structural flaws appear in the failure to match mission with capability with respect to the GCCs, as highlighted by FitzGerald and Wright. The difficulty in synchronizing cyber efforts with GCC requirements likely needs to be addressed to maximize the impact of cyber operations in support of GCC objectives. While maintaining the current structure may be easiest from a funding and turmoil perspective, it may be insufficient to meet requirements.

1.   Comparison of Modified Joint Structure to Current Structure

Adapting the current structure of USCYBERCOM to align under a USSOCOM C2 model could alleviate at least some portion of the issues with C2 of cyber forces. Interaction with the GCCs would likely improve, forces would likely be more responsive

---

[97] Tanner, "A Cyber Force for U.S. Cyberspace Operations", 2; "Roles in the Corps," accessed February 16, 2015, http://www.marines.com/being-a-marine/roles-in-the-corps/aviation-combat-element/fixed-wing-pilot; "Our Mission."

[98] Tanner, "A Cyber Force for U.S. Cyberspace Operations," 1–2.

to tasking, and training and education of cyber personnel could be streamlined and standardized to fulfill joint service needs. As opposed to creating an entirely new branch of service, modifying C2 of cyber forces would be far less disruptive to current operations.

Whether such a change would be sufficient to solve current issues would need to be further studied to determine if sufficient benefit can be gained by doing so. While not as disruptive as creating a new branch of service, there would likely be at least temporary disruption with respect to cyber support to the GCCs. If USCYBERCOM were to become a functional COCOM in the mold of USSOCOM, it would require additional funding, a difficult proposition in a time of defense budget and personnel cuts. Additionally, removing any level of the services' authority over its cyber personnel would surely be met with resistance, although that would not be insurmountable. Finally, C2 structure changes will have little impact without delegation of authority over cyber operations to the GCCs. Given the tightly controlled nature of cyber operations, barring a significant change in thought with regard to authorities, such delegation is unlikely any time soon.

2.   Comparison of Stand-Alone Force Structure to Current Structure

By creating such a force, many of the C2 issues highlighted by FitzGerald and Wright, as well as Hathaway, could be overcome. By having its own funding stream, a U.S. Cyber Force would be free to pursue new and disruptive technologies, much like the USAF after its founding. It could adjust its workforce as it saw fit, and rapidly integrate new training tools and techniques to maximize developments in the cyber field.

Transition to a stand-alone force would be the most disruptive option of all, and likely, would incur the greatest bureaucratic fallout. With steady or declining defense budgets projected into the future, one of the only growth areas is for cyber operations. The individual services, having spent time, personnel, and resources to populate their cyber ranks, would likely balk at divesting themselves of the cyber mission set. This resistance and sunk-cost argument should not end the debate regarding a cyber force, but it is still an obstacle. As in the case of making USCYBERCOM a functional COCOM similar in nature to USSOCOM, the authorities issue would again make the decentralization of cyber operations in support of GCC and national needs every bit as difficult for a U.S. Cyber Force. Finally, many of the benefits of a stand-alone force mirror the benefits garnered by creating a functional COCOM, rendering the utility of a stand-alone C2 structure roughly equivalent, and likely at greater cost.

F.   SUMMARY

The question of whether a need exists to create a cyber force separate from the other services is one that will likely be a continued point of debate for the foreseeable future. Although the decision to execute the cyber mission as a joint force has already been made, Chapter II shows that the growing importance of a new domain can eventually lead to the creation of a force dedicated solely to that domain. The effectiveness of USCYBERCOM's execution of its mission in the years ahead will be a major factor that determines whether it will continue as constructed, or be subject to drastic structural change as the newest branch of the U.S. military, the U.S. Cyber Force.

By understanding the available C2 structures for cyber forces, decision makers can tailor C2 of cyber forces to maximize the unique characteristics of such a force. The examination of the three models presented gives insight into their value as models for cyber C2 structure.

Chapter V offers a conclusion to this thesis. It also provides several topics for further study and consideration with respect to C2 of U.S. military cyber forces.

THIS PAGE INTENTIONALLY LEFT BLANK

V. CONCLUSION AND FUTURE WORK

A. CONCLUSION

This thesis examined historical analogies for U.S. military organization in new warfare domains, and explored three different C2 structures currently in use or that could be applied to cyber. By examining how the DOD organized to fight in air and space, this thesis provides context for why the cyber mission became one entrusted to a joint force, and why creation of a stand-alone force could occur.

As the history of air and space operations has shown, it is unlikely that USCYBERCOM will remain as is over time. Change will likely occur, and the C2 structure that commands cyber forces will evolve to fit the needs of the DOD. Regardless of which C2 structure is ultimately chosen for cyber forces, by changing policy to grant greater operational freedom to the command element of the nation's cyber forces, USCYBERCOM will be better positioned to fulfill its support mission to the GCCs. Whether a new branch of service is the result, as with the USAF, or in a modified joint structure, policymakers must be prepared to adapt C2 of DOD cyber forces.

B. FUTURE WORK

Due to the constantly evolving nature of the cyber domain, there will likely be changes forthcoming with respect to the DOD cyber force structure. Suggested areas for further research include: 1) study to determine the effectiveness, or lack thereof, of the current C2 structure, 2) further examination of cyber force C2 structure and relationships with the COCOMs if USCYBERCOM were to become its own functional COCOM, 3) further examination of how to build and structure a dedicated U.S. Cyber Force should a decision be made to create such a force, 4) legal and policy limitations of creating a dedicated cyber force within the DOD, and 5) the implications of the recent U.S. Naval War College Global 2014 war game, which tested a Joint Force Information Component Commander (JFICC) within the Joint Force Commander (JFC) construct to oversee all information-related missions, including space and cyber issues.[99] The final report highlighted the benefits realized from having an information component commander to oversee the broad array of technical capabilities, and that commander having the ability to integrate those capabilities into the broader campaign.

---

[99] Don Marrin and Walter Berbrick, *U.S. Naval War College Global 2014: Game Report* (Newport, RI: Naval War College, 2015), https://www.usnwc.edu/getattachment/Research---Gaming/War-Gaming/Documents/Publications/Game-Reports/Global-13-Game-Report.pdf.aspx.

LIST OF REFERENCES

Alexander, David. "Pentagon to Treat Cyberspace as "Operational Domain." *Reuters*, July 14, 2011. http://www.reuters.com/article/2011/07/14/us-usa-defense-cybersecurity-idUSTRE76D5FA20110714.

Arnold, Hap. "Memo for Chief of Staff of the Army, December 4, 1945." In Herman S. Wolk. *Planning and Organizing the Postwar Air Force: 1943–1947*. Washington, DC: United States Air Force, Office of Air Force History, 1984.

Bell, William Gardner. *Secretaries of War and Secretaries of the Army: Portraits and Biographical Sketches*. Washington, DC: Center of Military History, 2010.

Boehm, Joshua, Craig Baker, Stanley Chan, and Mel Sakazaki. "A History of United States National Security Space Management and Operations." Federation of American Scientists. Accessed March 10, 2015. http://fas.org/spp/eprint/article03.html#22.

Business Insurance. "U.S. Needs to Construct National Cyber Security Policy." February 15, 2015. http://www.businessinsurance.com/article/20150215/NEWS06/302159999/u-s-needs-to-construct-national-cyber-security-policy?tags=%7C302.

Chairman of the Joint Chiefs of Staff. *Joint Publication 3–05, Special Operations*. Washington, DC: Joint Chiefs of Staff, 2014.

Cinnamon, John D. *U.S. Department of the Space Force: A Necessary Evolution*. Norfolk, VA: Joint Forces Staff College, 2012.

Department of Defense. *Joint Operational Access Concept (JOAC)*. Washington, DC: Department of Defense, 2012. http://www.defense.gov/pubs/pdfs/JOAC_Jan%202012_Signed.pdf.

———. "Organizing and Managing for the Future." In *Report of the Commission to Assess United States National Security Space Management and Organization*. Ch. VI, 79–98. Washington, DC: Department of Defense, 2001. http://www.dod.mil/pubs/spaceabout.html.

———. "The Cyber Domain: Security and Operations." Accessed February 16, 2015. http://www.defense.gov/home/features/2013/0713_cyberdomain/.

———. Department of Defense Comptroller. "United States Department of Defense Fiscal Year 2015 Budget Request Overview." Accessed March 12, 2015. http://comptroller.defense.gov/Portals/45/Documents/defbudget/fy2015/fy2015_Budget_Request_Overview_Book.pdf.

————. Department of Defense Directive 5030.18. "DOD Support of National Aeronautics and Space Administrations." In Joshua Boehm, Craig Baker, Stanley Chan, and Mel Sakazaki. "A History of United States National Security Space Management and Operations." Federation of American Scientists. Accessed March 10, 2015. http://fas.org/spp/eprint/article03.html#22.

Dillon, Connie. "Air Force Space Command's Roots Traced Back to the 1940s." Air Force Space Command, December 10, 2012. http://www.spacedaily.com/reports/Air_Force_Space_Commands_roots_traced_back_to_the_1940s_999.html.

Economist, The. "Cyberwar: War in the Fifth Domain." July 1, 2010. http://www.economist.com/node/16478792.

Encyclopedia Britannica. "The First ICMBs." Accessed March 11, 2015. http://www.britannica.com/EBchecked/topic/1357360/rocket-and-missile-system/57336/The-first-ICBMs.

FitzGerald, Ben, and Parker Wright. *Digital Theaters: Decentralizing Cyber Command and Control.* Washington, DC: Center for a New American Security, 2014. http://www.cnas.org/sites/default/files/publications-pdf/CNAS_DigitalTheaters_FitzGeraldWright.pdf.

Fleet Air Arm Archive. "Naval Aviation History and Fleet Air Arm Origins: History of Naval Aviation of the Royal Navy and the Commonwealth." Accessed March 11, 2015. http://fleetairarmarchive.net/History/Index.htm.

Fort Gordon Public Affairs Office. "Army Cyber Branch Offers Soldiers New Challenges, Opportunities." November 24, 2014. http://www.army.mil/article/138883/Army_Cyber_branch_offers_Soldiers_new_challenges__opportunities/.

Gates, Robert M. *Establishment of a Subordinate Unified U.S. Cyber Command Under U.S. Strategic Command for Military Cyberspace Operations.* Secretary of Defense Memorandum. Washington, DC: Department of Defense, 2009.

GlobalSecurity.org. "United States Space Command." Accessed January 30, 2015. http://www.globalsecurity.org/space/agency/usspacecom.htm.

Harter, Mark E. "Ten Propositions Regarding Space Power: The Dawn of a Space Force." *Air & Space Power Journal*, Summer 2006.

Hathaway, David C. *Digital Kasserine Pass: The Battle over Command and Control of DOD's Cyber Forces.* Washington, DC: Brookings Institute, 2011.

Kaufman, Marc, and Dafna Linzer. "China Criticized for Anti-Satellite Missile Test." *Washington Post*, January 20, 2007. http://www.washingtonpost.com/wp-dyn/content/article/2007/01/18/AR2007011801029.html.

Marrin, Don, and Walter Berbrick. *U.S. Naval War College Global 2014: Game Report.* Newport, RI: Naval War College, 2015. https://www.usnwc.edu/getattachment/ Research---Gaming/War-Gaming/Documents/Publications/Game-Reports/Global-13-Game-Report.pdf.aspx.

Maurer, Maurer, ed. *The U.S. Air Service in World War I.* Washington, DC: United States Air Force, Office of Air Force History, 1978.

Military.com. "U.S. Armed Forces Overview." Accessed March 9, 2015. http://www. military.com/join-armed-forces/us-military-overview.html

Ministry of Defense. "Royal Air Force History: World War I." Accessed March 12, 2015. http://www.raf.mod.uk/history/ww1.cfm.

Moncrief, William S. "Building a United States Space Force." *Army Space Journal,* Winter/Spring 2010.

National Aeronautics and Space Administration. "Mercury: MR-3." Accessed January 6, 2015. http://www-pao.ksc.nasa.gov/kscpao/history/mercury/mr-3/mr-3.htm.

———. "Sounding Rockets." Accessed March 10, 2015. http://history.nasa.gov/SP-4402/ch5.htm.

———. "The First United States Satellite and Space Launch Vehicle." Accessed January 6, 2015. http://history.nasa.gov/sputnik/expinfo.html.

Obama, Barack H. *National Space Policy of the United States of America.* Washington, DC: The White House, 2010. http://www.whitehouse.gov/sites/default/files/nat ional_space_policy_6-28-10.pdf.

Peebles, Curtis. *High Frontier: The United States Air Force and the Military Space Program* Air Force History and Museums Program. Washington, DC: Air Force History Support Office, 1997. In Joshua Boehm, Craig Baker, Stanley Chan, and Mel Sakazaki. "A History of United States National Security Space Management and Operations." Federation of American Scientists. Accessed March 10, 2015. http://fas.org/spp/eprint/article03.html#22.

Pellerin, Cheryl. "Marines Focused at Tactical Edge of Cyber, Commander Says." U.S. Department of Defense, June 10, 2013. http://www.defense.gov/news/newsarticle. aspx?id=120246.

Pena, Paul J. "Evolving Threats Demand an Evolving National Security Strategy." *Forbes,* February 19, 2015. http://www.forbes.com/sites/realspin/2015/02/ 19/evolving-threats-demand-an-evolving-national-security-strategy/.

Sanborn, Morgan W. "National Military Space Doctrine." *Air University Review*, January–February 1977. http://www.airpower.maxwell.af.mil/airchronicles/ aureview/1977/jan-feb/sanborn.html.

Stavridis, James G. "Sailing the Cyber Seas." *Joint Forces Quarterly*, no. 65 (2nd Quarter 2012): 61–67. http://www.csl.army.mil/SLET/mccd/CyberSpacePubs/ Sailing%20the%20Cyber%20Sea.pdf.

Stavridis, James G., and David Weinstein. "Divide and Conquer: Why Dual Authority at the NSA and Cyber Command Hurts U.S. Security." *Foreign Affairs*, October 23, 2013. http://www.foreignaffairs.com/articles/140206/james-g-stavridis-and-dave-weinstein/divide-and-conquer.

———. "Time for a U.S. Cyber Force." *Proceedings Magazine*. Accessed January 10, 2015. http://www.usni.org/magazines/proceedings/2014-01/time-us-cyber-force.

Stewart, Richard W., ed. *American Military History Volume I: The United States Army and the forging of a Nation, 1775–1917*. Washington, DC: Center of Military History, 2005.

Story, Kurt S. *A Separate Space Force: An Old Debate with Renewed Relevance*. Carlisle Barracks, PA: U.S. Army War College, 2002.

Tanner, Leah. "A Cyber Force for U.S. Cyberspace Operations." Unpublished manuscript, September 17, 2014.

U.S. Air Force. "24th Air Force Fact Sheet." Accessed October 17, 2014. http://new preview.afnews.af.mil/24af/library/factsheets/factsheet.asp?id=15663.

———."Air Force Space Command Fact Sheet." Accessed March 12, 2015. http://www. afspc.af.mil/library/factsheets/factsheet.asp?id=3649.

———. "History, Part 1." Accessed February 16, 2015, http://www.airforce.com/learn-about/history/part1/.

———. "Our Mission." Accessed September 15, 2014. http://www.airforce.com/learn-about/our-mission/.

———. "Snapshot of the Air Force." U.S. Air Force Personnel Center. Accessed February 5, 2015. http://www.afpc.af.mil/library/airforcepersonneldemo graphics.asp.

———. "United States Air Force: Fiscal Year 2016 Budget Overview." Accessed March 12, 2015. http://www.saffm.hq.af.mil/shared/media/document/AFD-150210-043.pdf.

———. "USCYBERCOMMAND Cyber Mission Force." Accessed January 31, 2015. http://www.safcioa6.af.mil/shared/media/document/AFD-140512-039.pdf.

U.S. Army. "U.S. Army Aviation Timeline." Accessed January 5, 2015. http://www.army.mil/aviation/timeline/index.html.

———. *Army Regulation 95–5, Army Air Forces*. Washington, DC: United States Army, 1941. In Herman S. Wolk, *Planning and Organizing the Postwar Air Force: 1943–1947*. Washington, DC: United States Air Force, Office of Air Force History, 1984.

———. "Army Space Personnel Development Office Fact Sheet." Accessed March 12, 2015. http://www.smdc.army.mil/FactSheets/ASPDO.pdf.

U.S. Army Cyber Command. "Establishment of U.S. Army Cyber Command." Accessed October 17, 2014. http://www.arcyber.army.mil/history_arcyber.html.

U.S. Department of State. *Treaty on Principles Governing the Activities of States in the Exploration and Use of Outer Space, Including the Moon and Other Celestial Bodies*. Washington, DC: Department of State, 1967. http://www.state.gov/www/global/arms/treaties/space1.html.

U.S. Fleet Cyber Command/U.S. Tenth Fleet. *U.S. Fleet Cyber Command/U.S. 10th Fleet 2014 Fact Sheet*. Ft. Meade, MD: U.S. Fleet Cyber Command/U.S. Tenth Fleet, 2014. http://www.public.navy.mil/fcc-c10f/Fact%20Sheets/FCC-C10F%20Fact%20Sheet%202014.pdf.

U.S. History.com. "Secretaries of the Navy." Accessed March 10, 2015. http://www.u-s-history.com/pages/h1225.html http://www.u-s-history.com/pages/h1225.html.

U.S. Marine Corps. "Roles in the Corps." Accessed February 16, 2015. http://www.marines.com/being-a-marine/roles-in-the-corps/aviation-combat-element/fixed-wing-pilot.

U.S. Navy. "Navy Organization." Accessed October 16, 2014. http://www.navy.mil/navydata/organization/org-top.asp.

———. Office of the Deputy Chief of Naval Operations for Information Dominance (N2/N6). "Navy Space Cadre." August 6, 2014. http://www.doncio.navy.mil/chips/ArticleDetails.aspx?ID=5356.

U.S. Special Operations Command. *USSOCOM Fact Book 2012*. MacDill AFB, FL: U.S. Special Operations Command, 2012. http://www.socom.mil/News/Documents/USSOCOM_Fact_Book_2012.pdf.

———. *USSOCOM Fact Book 2014*. MacDill AFB, FL: U.S. Special Operations Command, 2014. http://www.socom.mil/News/Documents/USSOCOM_Fact_Book_2014.pdf.

U.S. Strategic Command. "History." Accessed March 12, 2015. http://www.stratcom.mil/history/.

———. "Joint Functional Component Command for Space (JFCC Space)." Accessed January 30, 2015. http://www.stratcom.mil/factsheets/7/JFCC_Space/.

USSTRATCOM. "Mission." Accessed March 12, 2015. http://www.stratcom.mil/mission/.

———. "U.S. Cyber Command." Accessed October 11, 2014. http://www.stratcom.mil/factsheets/2/Cyber_Command/.

Vandenberg AFB Public Affairs. "Joint Functional Component Command for Space." March 15, 2013. http://www.vandenberg.af.mil/library/factsheets/factsheet.asp?id=12579.

Wolk, Herman S. *Planning and Organizing the Postwar Air Force: 1943–1947*. Washington, DC: United States Air Force, Office of Air Force History, 1984.

———. *Reflections on Air Force Independence*. Washington, DC: Air Force History Support Office, 2007.

———. *The Struggle for Air Force Independence: 1943–1947*, Washington, DC: Air Force History and Museums Program, 1997.

———. *Toward Independence: The Emergence of the U.S. Air Force 1945–1947*. Washington, DC: Air Force History Support Office, 1996.

www.ingramcontent.com/pod-product-compliance
Lightning Source LLC
Chambersburg PA
CBHW060444060326
40690CB00019B/4328